Artificial Sweetness

poems by

Charles K. Carter

Finishing Line Press
Georgetown, Kentucky

Artificial Sweetness

Copyright © 2023 by Charles K. Carter
ISBN 979-8-88838-300-1 First Edition
All rights reserved under International and Pan-American Copyright Conventions. No part of this book may be reproduced in any manner whatsoever without written permission from the publisher, except in the case of brief quotations embodied in critical articles and reviews.

ACKNOWLEDGMENTS

Thank you to these literary journals and presses who originally published versions of the following poems:

The Broadkill Review: "Time Bending" "Tongue"
Door is a Jar Magazine: "Crushed"
Emerge Literary Journal: "Uncoiled"
Fahmidan Journal: "Hate Crime"
The Hellebore: "Inventory"
The Jupiter Review: "Vantage Point"
Lazy Adventurer Publishing: "Desperation" "Jealous"
One Art: "Omen"
Resurrection Magazine: "The A-to-Z's of Losing You"
Reunion: The Dallas Review: "If You Change Your Mind"

"If You Change Your Mind" references the ABBA song "Take a Chance on Me."

As always, Brandon Carter, thank you for being my number one, my cheerleader, my rock.

Aurora Bones, thank you for all of your help workshopping these poems.
Thank you, Theresa Davis, along with Java Speaks and The Arts Xchange for providing opportunities to share these pieces along their journeys.
Last, but certainly not least, thank you to everyone at Finishing Line Press for helping bring this project to life!

Publisher: Leah Huete de Maines
Editor: Christen Kincaid
Cover Art: Brandon Carter
Author Photo: Charles K. Carter
Cover Design: Brandon Carter and Charles K. Carter

Order online: www.finishinglinepress.com
also available on amazon.com

Author inquiries and mail orders:
Finishing Line Press
PO Box 1626
Georgetown, Kentucky 40324
USA

Table of Contents

Ode to the Straight Boy Who Acted Gay in High School 1
Sleepovers 2
What Was Said 3
Documentation 4
Shapeshifter 5
Tongue 6
Hate Crime 7
What Was Unsaid 8
Play Thing 9
Crushed 10
Surgeon General's Warning: 11
Red-Penned Revisions 12
Making 13
If You Change Your Mind 14
The Fitting 15
Artificial Sweetness 16
What Was 17
Crumbling 18
Desperation 19
Hunted 20
What a Heart was Supposed to Sound Like 21
Protection Spell 22
The Difference 23
His Gentle Hands 24
Jealous 25
Shrine 26
Omen 27
Vantage Point 28
The A-to-Z's of Losing You 29
Uncoiled 31
Time Bending 32
Inventory 33

Ode to the Straight Boy Who Acted Gay in High School

Your salty satire showed me what was possible,
what was unnamed in my warming vessels.

You taught me what was sacred.
You denied deviating from what was *natural*,

claiming it was all an act
but then one Thursday night at confirmation class,

you sat next to me, your forefinger wrestled my waistline for bare skin
before tracing lightning into these hips.

Sleepovers

He had a cartoon-sized block head
and the habit of doing The Rock eyebrow raises every five minutes.
This was back when The Rock was only a wrestler.
We would rent R-rated movies from the local video store
that specifically claimed to have nudity.
His eyes were glued
as the unknown actress's large breasts bounced like gelatin molds
while my eyes held onto Matthew Davis' thrusting glutes.
If you paused the DVD at the right moment,
you could see Colin Farrell's package.
It worked to get us both going.
He was only okay with brief strokes with fists or tongues
while I wanted to take it further.
This was just experimentation to him
but for me, the awakening of a deeper craving.

What Was Said

Text me *sometime,*
he says with a sharp smile.
Or I'll reach out to you,
whatever.

Documentation

I screenshot his nice
words so I can look back,
believe in love again.

Shapeshifter

I think it's something to do
with the whites of the dog's eyes.
Most dogs' eyes are brown
and typically you only see these full dark orbs.

Sometimes they look
more like the eyes of an alien
or a shark than a human's.

But humans can give those puppy dog eyes too.
Sometimes they give them when they don't even notice,
like when you're creeping on this guy-you-like's socials,
looking at his cute face,
like when you're falling in love with said guy
and all his silly dance moves,
like when he tries to lie his way out of his wandering affections.

But what do you do when he finds someone else
and you are haunted by his puppy dog eyes,
his softness,
his humanness?

How do you ignore the whites in his eyes
or the dimples when he smiles?

How do you view him as less canine
and more shark?

Tongue

I am drawn to you
like my tongue is drawn
to the gap between my teeth
—there's no good reason but it fits
and it feels right against my sharp edges.

Hate Crime

I read you
reading me: untranslated text in a language
we both should know
    We skipped history class for this?

(I need you)
house on fire, shattered mirror,
overflowing car ashtray
    There's room for one more, right?

(I love you)
brick through window
shattered shards of glittering glass
    How did someone find us here?

I left you
scared and afraid
bleeding angel wings in the backseat
    Did our last kiss count as a goodbye?

What Was Unsaid

____ __ _____ ,¹
__ ___ ___ __ ___ ___ .²
__ ___ ___ __ __ __ ,³
____ .⁴

Play Thing

You coddled me lovingly and delicately
—until you didn't,
until your fondness
grew dust bunnies under the bed.

Stitches pulled apart until
I am an open sore taking in all
the darkness and wetness
of your own kissing wounds.

You said you cleaned me up
and pieced me back together
but this does not look like me,
this does not feel a thing like me.

I curse you, tear myself open,
and let the rain wash away
this polished image of me
you crafted in your pretty head.

I do not belong as recycled art
crafted by the hands of a god
but instead the original ruins
created when you loved me.

Crushed

You plucked a cigarette from my pack
and placed it between your plump lips,
using your own lighter to ignite.
We stood on your balcony,
without pants, mid-coitus.
We needed a break from the heat.
The chill in the fall air
raised the hairs on my thighs.
You leaned on the rail,
looking out into the sky
like you had found the answer
to one of life's many mysteries.
I looked across the street
at the vacant playground equipment
of a vacant pre-school—
empty swings, forgotten joy.
For a moment, our conversation
was as raw and naked as we were.
We talked about trauma
and about anxiety medications.
But then you rattled on about video games
before crushing your cigarette butt
in the vintage orange glass ashtray
before taking me by the hand,
leading me back inside
to finish what we had started.

Surgeon General's Warning:

Men exaggerate
fishing tales, their cock size, and
how much they love you.

Red-Penned Revisions

I was an uncorrected proof
until he started correcting me
with red raging pen
and now I don't quite recognize
the syntax in my own cries for help.

Making

Like removing
grapefruit peel from its flesh
make my juices drip
down your finger
make my scent
sing out
into the night breeze

create blues.

If You Change Your Mind

Hi, my name is Charlie and I am recovering from trauma.
My recovery often shows up in my romantic life.

When I start talking to a new guy,
I almost instantly imagine his arms like tree limbs
providing me with shelter from the rain,
like an abandoned tree house in the woods
where we can escape the world.

I picture his smile
as a safe house for my battered heart,
that my heart, a drum constantly beating for war,
could match his soft rhythm and find some solace.

I fantasize about our touch,
moving beyond hand-holding and horseplay
to that of a gentle vulnerable caress, the mellow spring breeze
pressing its tender lips against our naked bodies.

But this isn't *Brokeback Mountain*,
we aren't running around naked in the woods.
This isn't *Latter Days*
where love cures all and saves the day.
This isn't *Call Me By Your Name*
where we at least have a sizzling summer romance
to warm our middle-age.

No, this is me, making up a fairy tale
in which I don't belong.

It's me giving him a houseplant when he moves apartments.
It's me attaching a note with an ABBA lyric,
If you change your mind...
It's me wondering if the houseplant is still alive.

It's me wondering if he ever remembered that I was first in line.

The Fitting
after Aurora Bones

Sometimes loving you
is like a child playing with a shape sorter,

trying to fit a heart through an open circle wound.
It doesn't fit but I keep trying my best to make it fit,

smashing my heart to smithereens.

Artificial Sweetness

She eats grape jelly
straight from the jar,
as if she can spoon out
a little sweetness
to take the bitter
out of her days.

What Was

1. I will. Three times. Appropriate wait time between each jagged attempt. No reply.
2. That cuts me in my dreams. Leaves me covered in sweat.
3. He won't.
4. Forget everything else he ever said. What he actually meant.

Crumbling

You can tell a lot about a person
by their cookie preference.

He is confident, solid

—while I am unfulfilled, soft,
undercooked; ready to fall
apart with the slightest touch.

Desperation

Desperation is
an ugly sweater that don't
look good on me.
Come on home to me, my love,
and strip me of this
jealousy.

Hunted

I.
Last Saturday
a small bird flew into our broken window
and fell between the panes.

She was being hunted by a hawk.
When the hawk realized he was unable to grab her,
he flew to a nearby tree to perch and wait for her escape.

The little bird tried and cried to free herself
but the space between the panes was too restricting
to permit liftoff, especially for a novice aviator.

My husband watched until the hawk flew off.
Then he went outside, grabbed a stick and stuck it between
the window panes, creating an escape route.

He stepped back
and allowed her to hop up the twig
before finding sweet freedom in the autumn air.

II.
I am often trapped
by my own insecurities hunting me down day-after-day.
And he is gentle. He is kind. He is reassuring butterfly kisses.

He gives me light-up emergency exit signs to his arms,
a way to crawl out of my own misery
but I am too afraid to scale these tall fortress walls.

These walls were built to protect me,
to save me from any more hurt,
to shield me from any more shame.

I don't know how to tear them down.
I don't know if I can.
I don't know if I can.

What a Heart was Supposed to Sound Like

I have a broken heart and that's not figurative poetic bullshit,
that's a literal description.
You noticed it the first time you lay your head upon my chest,
hypnotized by the broken lub dub.
Moments turned into minutes, months, and years
and you expressed the desire to dance only to this rhythm
for the rest of your life.

You don't like to think about it, this broken heart,
but you've accompanied me to enough white coat visits,
you've seen the EKGs.

You don't like to think about it,
how blood heats with acids, coagulates, and anchors sinking ships
and one day that day will come
when this broken heart will drop a beat no more.

And I want you to take care of my cat
and here is a book I want you to read on Christmas Eve
and think about me.

Protection Spell

When we move
into our first house,
he hangs roses
from the crown molding, casts
a protection spell
in the four cardinal directions.

Are we safe now
from the shadowman?

The Difference

He says he will show up when he shows up,
they will be lucky to have his company.

I wish I had his confidence.

I show up early with compliments and wine,
hoping for validation for all the space I take up.

His Gentle Hands
    for Babycakes

I watch him
guard the rabbit nest from the dogs.

I watch him
fence the nest when he mows, to carefully avoid their soft bodies.

I watch him
cautiously relocate them to safety when they are old enough to leave
    the nest.

I watch him
in his gentle ways and he reminds me there is love in this world,

pure and unrestricted at its source.

Jealous

dusk falls on the city,
feet stumble for footing,
hands fumble for fingers,
lips search for other lips.
the truck won't start again,
we will have to walk home.
tonight, they will drive by
jealous of our quiet
love, as the moon watches
the stars, how they kiss the
bright eyes of god.

Shrine

On anniversaries and birthdays,
we buy and create art for the walls:

> *I love you more*
> *Cute as a button*
> *Always kiss me goodnight*

A decade in and our bedroom has become a cocoon,
a shrine of loving affirmations to wake up every day to:

> *You are my sunshine*
> *You light up my life*
> *I can't help falling in love with you*

The morning sun beams through our white lace curtains.
I kiss the muted sunshine resting softly on your shoulders:

> *Je t'aime mon papillon*

Grow you wings.

Omen

A framed photograph
from our first anniversary celebration
fell off the wall.

I put it back up
but it fell again,
this time on your precious head.

The frame was held up
both times by overpriced Velcro strips
that promised no damage.

They vowed
to hold this weight.

Vantage Point

I swerve to miss the toddler's ball as his mother wrestles him out of
 his booster seat
for the quick rest-stop-hustle. I take a sharp right around an out-of-
 order gas pump,

out of the way of the toy. I do not stop, though. I do not rescue the
 child from a maybe-grief.
I do not rescue the mother from that headache of a screaming child
 the rest of the way home.

I keep on driving because I have a hard enough time wrestling the
 need to save myself.
But I feel your eyes penetrating me from the passenger seat, judging
 me.

And I feel like a villain in a superhero comic, a two-dimensional
 queer-coded
bad guy with bad teeth, bad posture, and no redeeming backstory.

The A-to-Z's of Losing You

Appetizers split at Applebee's.
Banana Everclear shots.
Chipotle.
Daytime drives.
Evening snuggles.
Fast Friday morning fucks.
Grinding with some guy from Grindr.
Heavenly, time-stands-still hugs.
Ignoring each other's faults and sometimes cries for help.
Joking at funerals.
Kisses galore.
Laughing at comedy specials together.
Moving apartments tests a relationship.
Naps.
Open dialogue about open relationships.
Picking stuck celery out of my teeth for me.
Queer marches, queer votes, queer revolution.
Reading each other's lips, eyes, and poetry.
Sitting side by side when there are no words.
Tucking you in when you are sick.
Unbuttoning, unzipping, undoing.
Various artists on various mix tapes on various road trips.
Wet Premium Lubricant.
X-rays, surgeries, and other hospital visits.
Yellow dining room walls.
Zzzs lost when we were up all night binge-watching *Buffy the Vampire Slayer*.

All these memories remain, leaving me feeling:

Ambivalent.
Bitter.
Crippled.
Damaged goods that can't be returned.
Earring missing its match.
Fast Friday morning fucks ups.

Grinding with some guy from Grindr.
Health food can go to hell.
Ice cream helps.
Jumping thoughts.
Kisses somehow remain on my lips.
Lips yearning for your skin.
Moving out is easier than moving on.
Naps—lots of naps.
Open heart, broken, but still open.
Picking up glass from broken picture frames.
Quiet cremation of old pictures.
Reading your texts again way too many times.
Searching for clues, searching for answers.
Tucking a few memories in the bottom of a box.
Unraveling.
Various artists sing sad songs to me.
Wet pillowcases from tears.
X-rays can't be done on broken hearts.
Yellow walls must be painted back to white before we get our deposit back.
Zzzs lost when I lost you.

Uncoiled

> *"If uncoiled, the DNA in all the cells in your body would stretch 10 billion miles—from here to Pluto and back."*
> Discover Magazine

you gifted melodies
of pop standards to my ears,
eyes all starry while singing
frank sinatra's "fly me to the moon."
but we could go farther than that.
you took me on a trip to the stars,
loosened my anxiety's grip,
gently uncoiled me to my fullest self,
overflowing dipper of milk.
we joined into one celestial body,
untangling our demons and ghosts
until we were astronauts headed for
jupiter's icy rings
and then onto some goldilocks orb
in a galaxy far, far away.

we were fueled by the naïve hope of young love.
we were adventurers.
we were astronauts.

we *were* astronauts.

now,
i am just a lovesick fool,
half the man i used to be.
i thought i could remedy
this ache by wallowing
in the red planet's haze
but now i am a ball of melancholy,
a child's bitter, sticky fist
barely able to slingshot
myself to the moon.

Time Bending

There is a meme
of the Godzilla movie
in reverse: a monster erecting a city
and then returning
to the sea.

Maybe I'm looking
at our relationship all wrong.
If I look at it backwards,
the bitterness in your eyes blossoms

into sweet, unbridled joy.

Inventory

All the Things I Love:

>Morning sex. Vegan nachos. Melissa Etheridge.
>Buddha. Band tees. Hash browns.
>Puppies. Joni Mitchell. Soft hair.
>Joy Harjo. Blue jeans. Vegan ice cream.
>Jesus. Bob Dylan. Whales.
>Alanis Morrissette. Fresh kiwi. Athletic shorts.
>Penguins. *Will & Grace*. Dimples.
>Gwen Hart. Denim jackets with patches. French fries.
>My mother. Andrea Gibson. The ocean.
>Mashed potatoes. Backs of hands. Thich Nhat Hanh.
>Mandarin oranges. Warm sand on my toes. The sunrise.
>Kayaking. The Used. *The Golden Girls*.
>Lips. Yoga. A ripe peach.
>A good laugh. Walking outdoors. Saeed Jones.
>HIM. Christmas morning. My sister.
>The Dalai Lama. My grandmother. Potato chips.
>Tree pose. Tall trees. Road trips.
>My Chemical Romance. Sister Helen Prejean. Silence.
>A good cry. Sweet Chili Doritos. My sophomore English teacher.
>Peace signs. Christmas music. Chipotle.
>But not you. Not you. Not you.

All the Things I Pretend Not to Love:

>You.

Charles K. Carter is a queer poet from Iowa. He shares his home with his artist husband and their spoiled pets. He enjoys film, yoga, and live music. Melissa Etheridge is his ultimate obsession. Carter holds an MFA in writing from Lindenwood University. His poems have appeared in numerous literary journals. He is the author of *Read My Lips* (David Robert Books) as well as several chapbooks.

Connect on Twitter, Facebook, and Instagram @CKCpoetry

www.CKCpoetry.com

www.ingramcontent.com/pod-product-compliance
Lightning Source LLC
Chambersburg PA
CBHW022124090426
42743CB00008B/991